LIFE **ON EARTH!**
Biodiversity Explained

FOREST
LIFE CONNECTIONS

By Raymond Bergin

BEARPORT
PUBLISHING

Minneapolis, Minnesota

Cover and title page, © iPGGutenbergUKLtd/iStock, © fun__Sherrins/iStock, © Oskan0v/ Stock, © K__Thalhofer/iStock, © Frank Cornelissen/iStock, © Jmrocek/iStock, © GlobalP/ Stock, and © Emils Vanags/iStock; 4–5, © Stéphane Bidouze/Adobe Stock, © Biletskiy Evgeniy/Adobe Stock, © ChooChin/iStock, and © estherpoon/iStock; 6–7, © Rod Hill/ Getty Images; 8, © Cheattha/Adobe Stock, © cosmln/iStock, © Issaurinko/iStock, © cosmln/iStock, and © Svetlana Zritneva/iStock; 9T, © mmac72/Getty Images; 9M, © Gary A Nelson/Dembinsky Photo Associates/Alamy; 9B, © dennisvdw/iStock; 10–11, © Christopher Milligan/Alamy; 12–13, © Christian Kober 1/Alamy; 14, © Kung__Mangkorn/iStock; 14–15, © somnuk krobkum/Getty Images; 17, © Leonide Principe/Alamy; 18–19, © Mark Castiglia/ Alamy; 20–21, © USFS Photo/Alamy; 22–23, © Monique van Someren/Getty Images; 24–25, © Kamil Hajek/Alamy; 26–27, © Anup Shah/Getty Images; 28, © Rawpixel.com/ Shutterstock; 29 step 1, © AzmanL/iStock; 29 step 2, © izusek/iStock; 29 step 3, © Elizabeth Lara/iStock; 29 step 4, © Maryviolet/iStock; and 29 step 5, © LeManna/iStock.

Bearport Publishing Company Product Development Team
President: Jen Jenson; Director of Product Development: Spencer Brinker; Senior Editor: Allison Juda; Editor: Charly Haley; Associate Editor: Naomi Reich; Senior Designer: Colin O'Dea; Associate Designer: Elena Klinkner; Associate Designer: Kayla Eggert; Product Development Assistant: Anita Stasson

Library of Congress Cataloging-in-Publication Data

Names: Bergin, Raymond, 1968- author.
Title: Forest life connections / by Raymond Bergin.
Description: Minneapolis, Minnesota : Bearport Publishing Company, [2023] | Series: Life on earth! Biodiversity explained | Includes bibliographical references and index.
Identifiers: LCCN 2022033642 (print) | LCCN 2022033643 (ebook) | ISBN 9798885094108 (library binding) | ISBN 9798885095327 (paperback) | ISBN 9798885096478 (ebook)
Subjects: LCSH: Forest biodiversity--Juvenile literature. | Forest ecology--Juvenile literature.
Classification: LCC QH86 .B3974 2023 (print) | LCC QH86 (ebook) | DDC 577.3--dc23/eng/20220829
LC record available at https://lccn.loc.gov/2022033642
LC ebook record available at https://lccn.loc.gov/2022033643

For more information, write to Bearport Publishing, 5357 Penn Avenue South, Minneapolis, MN 55419

Contents

A Tale of Two Forests

In the middle of a forest, tall trees shade bushes and shrubs. All around, there are signs of life. Birds soar above the treetops, and monkeys swing from branch to branch. Bees buzz among flowering plants near a stream teeming with fish.

But just downstream, there are many more dead stumps than towering trees. The sounds of bird calls, chattering monkeys, and buzzing bees are replaced with the rumble of trucks speeding along a nearby road. What's happening to life on Earth?

Even the dirt on the forest floor is packed with life. Just one teaspoon of healthy soil can hold more living organisms than there are people on the planet!

A Planet Full of Life

Earth is made up of **biomes**—areas of land and sea where the **climate** and natural features allow certain kinds of plants and animals to live together. Oceans, wetlands, tundras, grasslands, deserts, and forests are all biomes.

Every biome is home to a connected community of plant and animal life. This wide variety of life is called **biodiversity**. In a forest biome, it can include everything from tiny bacteria and bitty beetles to large mountain lions and towering redwoods.

Forests cover almost a third of the planet's land and are home to about 65 percent of its mammal **species**.

The Wide World of Forests

Different types of forests are home to different kinds of plants and animals. **Boreal** forests are located in cold, snowy places. Only trees and animals that can survive harsh winters live there. **Temperate** forests are found in places with milder climates where a larger variety of plants and animals can survive. **Tropical** rain forests are often warm and wet most of the year. They burst with even more life than temperate forests. In fact, these biomes can have 500 tree species packed into an area the size of two football fields!

One species of tree in Panama's tropical forests is home to more than a thousand kinds of beetles. A single Amazonian bush can have more ants than the number of people living in the state of New York.

Boreal forest

Temperate forest

Tropical forest

9

It All Fits Together

Each living thing within a forest plays a role in the survival of the biome and the rest of the life it contains. The animals and plants within biomes rely on one another for food, shelter, and protection. The Halloween crab digs burrows and shares them with insects and spiders. As it loosens the soil, the crab also helps plant roots grow, resulting in more food for **grazing** animals to eat and in turn more grazers for carnivores to consume.

However, when these life connections are disrupted, forest biomes become weaker. The community begins to break down.

Many forests have layers of life—different plants and creatures live along the forest floor, in the branches, and along the treetops. Life in each layer depends on the health of other layers.

Halloween crabs live in forests near the ocean.

Disappearing Forests

Surrounded by trees, scampering squirrels, and beautiful birdsong, it's easy to think Earth's forests are healthy. But they are actually at risk. Plants and animals in the forest are facing a changing climate.

Since 1990, the world has lost 1.6 million square miles (4.1 million sq km) of forest—an area six times the size of Texas! As the trees and other plants disappear, so do the birds, bugs, fish, and furry animals that live amongst them.

Tropical forests are disappearing especially fast. By some estimates, about a football field–sized area of rain forest disappears every six seconds.

Farm Harm

Many of the world's forests are cut down to make room for farmland. During this devastating **deforestation**, thousands of plant species are removed, often to make way for single-crop farming.

Sloths live in Central and South American forests. If the sloth disappears along with its leafy home, so will the millions of things living and growing in its fur.

Many tropical forests—and the more than 50,000 tree species they contain—are cleared to grow oil palm trees. Palm oil is a popular **ingredient** in baking and beauty products, but the cleared land doesn't support the animals that relied on the forest for food and shelter. Orangutans, chimpanzees, tigers, rhinos, and elephants have lost their homes and food sources. Many species now face **extinction**.

Trees without the Forest

Some of the farm crops that are planted in place of **native** plants struggle to survive due to the lack of biodiversity, too. Brazil nut tree **plantations** are pollinated by only one kind of rain forest bee. However, this bee needs the smell of a specific rain forest orchid to attract **mates**. Only one kind of rodent plants the nut tree's seeds, but this furry mammal eats the fruit of other forest trees to survive. Many Brazil nut plantations fail because farmers cleared away too much of the other forest life.

Brazil nut trees can be a part of healthy, diverse biomes. The trees offer shelter to the flying critters that pollinate the forest's fruit trees, which provide juicy fruit for other forest animals.

A Broken Home

Some large forests are broken up by areas of human development. This leads to **fragmentation**. For some animals, this can be just as harmful as complete deforestation.

The golden-headed lion tamarin of Brazil lives across a large area of tropical forest, with its food and shelter spread out far and wide. As farms, roads, and even cities cut up the tamarin's large territory, the animal is often separated from nesting areas and some of the food it needs to survive. Unable to reach every part of its forest home, the tamarin is put at risk.

Golden-headed lion tamarins are vital to the health of rain forests. They spit out seeds from the fruit they eat, spreading more than 70 kinds of fruit plants around the forest.

Forests on Fire

Many of the forests that aren't cut down are facing an ever-growing threat of burning instead. Normally, small wildfires are a natural part of forest life and can keep forest biomes healthy. However, temperatures around the globe are on the rise, making wildfires anything but normal.

Now, wildfires are burning more often, hotter, and for longer. The fires kill many trees and other plants. The animals that are too small or slow to escape die in the flames.

In 2019 and 2020, wildfires in Australian forests killed or displaced about 3 billion animals, including kangaroos, koalas, frogs, spiders, and dung beetles.

Higher temperatures dry out forest plants, making them easier to burn when a fire starts.

Uninvited Guests

Another way forest life is harmed is when new plants or animals that do not belong there move in. These **invasive** species can quickly take over a forest and kill off native creatures.

The emerald ash borer is an invasive beetle. The pest has killed hundreds of millions of ash trees, forcing birds and squirrels from their nests in the branches. Other insects that feed harmlessly on ash trees are going hungry as more and more trees die. The squirrels, mice, and ducks that fed on ash seeds must find other food sources, too.

An emerald ash borer

The emerald ash borer was originally from Asia. It was first discovered in North America in 2002. By 2018, it had spread across 35 U.S. states and 5 Canadian provinces.

People and Forests

Clearly, problems of the forests have wide-reaching impacts. Even humans are harmed when forests fail. Every day, we use forest plants and animals for our food, firewood, building supplies, and clothing. We get cancer-fighting drugs and other medicines from plants in the forests. When we harm our forests, we risk losing many of these natural resources. And—as we've learned—when one species goes, many more might follow. Our lives could literally depend on saving forest biodiversity.

Forests fight the warming that threatens all life on the planet. Each year, they absorb 17 billion tons (15 billion t) of heat-trapping **carbon dioxide**.

Bark from some trees can be used to make drugs that treat cancer.

Forest Life Returns

Many governments and organizations are trying to protect remaining forestlands and to stop further deforestation. Instead of clearing huge areas of forest for wood products, some are cutting down individual trees. This leaves a variety of trees to maintain the forest's biodiversity. Some are even replanting forests with native trees, which brings back the populations of the plants and animals that rely on those relationships to survive. When biodiversity is respected and protected, our planet really comes to life!

In 2007, foresters in Borneo planted 350,000 native trees, including many that bear the fruit that feed forest creatures. Since then, more than 1,000 animal species, 15,000 plant species, and 1,000 tree species have bounced back.

Borneo's orangutan population was especially helped by replanting efforts.

Save the Forest

Saving the forests and the life they contain seems like a huge job. But there are small, everyday steps we can take to protect forests and forest creatures from harm.

Reuse scrap paper and recycle used paper whenever possible. That way, fewer trees have to be cut down to make new paper.

Volunteer to help plant trees or clean up a forest near you.

When visiting forests, stay on marked paths and be sure to take any trash with you.

Start campfires only when there is a low risk of forest fires. Make sure all fires are fully put out when you're done with them.

Avoid burning fuel and using gas whenever possible and safe. If you can, walk, ride a bike, or take public transportation to get where you're going.

Glossary

biodiversity the existence of many different kinds of plants and animals in an environment

biomes regions with a particular climate and environment where certain kinds of plants and animals live

boreal related to parts of the world in colder northern regions

carbon dioxide a gas given off when fossil fuels are burned

climate the typical weather in a place

deforestation the clearing or loss of forests

extinction when a type of animal or plant dies out completely

fragmentation the act of breaking something up into pieces

grazing eating plants

ingredient one of the substances something is made from

invasive spreading in a place where something doesn't belong

mates animals that come together to have young

native originally belonging to a certain place

plantations large farms where crops are grown

species groups that animals and plants are divided into according to similar characteristics

temperate related to a part of the world with different seasons and few weather extremes compared to hot or cold climates

tropical related to parts of the world near the equator where the weather is very warm

Read More

Bergin, Raymond. *Fires Everywhere (What on Earth? Climate Change Explained).* Minneapolis: Bearport Publishing, 2022.

Eboch, M. M. *Forest Biomes Around the World (Exploring Earth's Biomes).* North Mankato, MN: Capstone Press, 2020.

Johnson, Rebecca L. *A Walk in the Boreal Forest (Biomes of North America), 2nd ed.* Minneapolis: Lerner Publications, 2021.

Learn More Online

1. Go to **www.factsurfer.com** or scan the QR code below.

2. Enter "**Forest Connections**" into the search box.

3. Click on the cover of this book to see a list of websites.

Index

About the Author

Raymond Bergin lives in New Jersey. Though it is the most densely human-populated state in the United States, at least 40 percent of the land is covered in forest. It is one of the country's most biodiverse states. In addition to forests, New Jersey includes oceans, wetlands, and grasslands.